murmur rumble roar

Other books by Nikki Tajiri

She Dreams When She Bleeds

poems about climate change

Murmur
Rumble
Roar

n i k k i t a j i r i

Printed by Kindle Direct Publishing
Illustrations and design by Nikki Tajiri

First printing, 2020

Published by Nikki Tajiri
Instagram @nikkitajiri
Email nik.tajiri@gmail.com

To our favorite places

I

TRANSGRESSIONS

First she murmured
Then she rumbled
Next she will roar

[Mother Earth]

Here we are
Hot getting hotter
Cold getting colder
Lands getting barer
Oceans getting emptier

We are all wondering
How could we do this
And keep doing this
To ourselves

The point we fell apart
Was the point where we said
You're on your own
You can stand alone
You must

Go compete for your little patch
Build your box
Fill it up with empty delights
And don't come back

[Independence]

Our lungs are on fire and
Our hands said who cares
I can't feel the heat

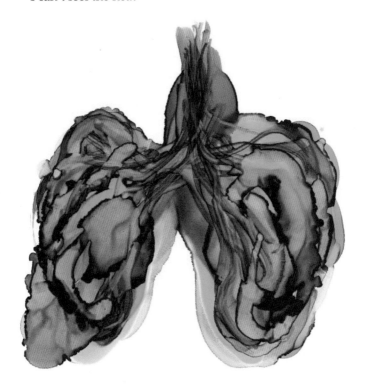

Find us at the corner
Of catastrophe
And confusion

[Current Location]

Scarcity is an opinion
Not a reality
There is enough to share

Scarcity is our collective choice
When we divide and we judge
When we uphold our arbitrary systems

Scarcity is never having enough
The parasite in all of us
That consumes until the host is dead

We think that
If something doesn't respond
Like a human
It's not intelligent

[Fallacy]

I feel it too
The anxiety the despair
My mind is spewing
Like the factories I imagine
The future lives in our heads

Come back to right now
Go outside
Let her hold you and
Surrender to the world around

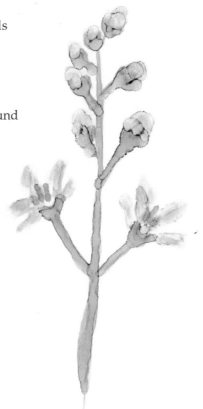

My poetry and my life
Are funded by fossil fuels

[Irony]

Our current situation is
A projection of
Our incessant need to do
Instead of to be

She is not
An inanimate object

[Objectified]

We can drown
In rising oceans
We can drown
In negativity too

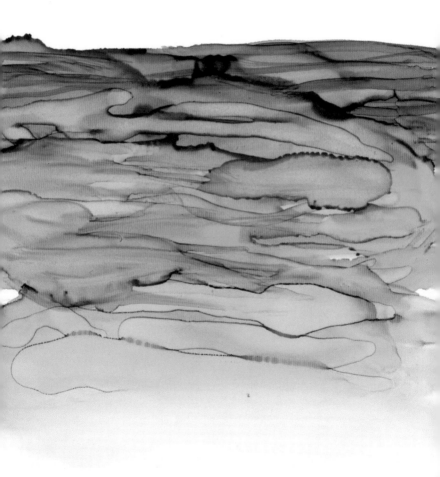

Abandon
Any system where
Leaving the land pristine
Results in a loss

[System Failure]

When did uncertainty
Become the enemy
When did growth
Become a necessity

We are the imposters
Who claim to love nature
While living
An indoor life

[Climate Controlled]

We can't buy love
But that doesn't
Stop us from trying

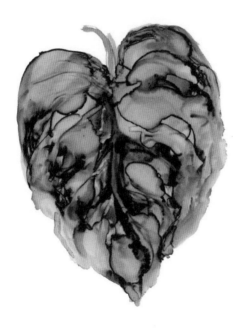

All these judgments
Are toxic too

[Sources of Pollution]

At the root of it all
Is our fear
Of what's next

II

TRANSFORMATION

Be not afraid to dismantle
The powers that be

Learn from
The ones who
Can hear her

[Indigenous]

Do not feel guilty
If you are not somehow
Actively sequestering carbon and
Heroically solving the crisis by
Inventing a new technology

We got into this mess
With a certain mindset
And so if you can change your mind
You're helping to lead us out

We need to make
A quick change
To a slow life

[Slow Down]

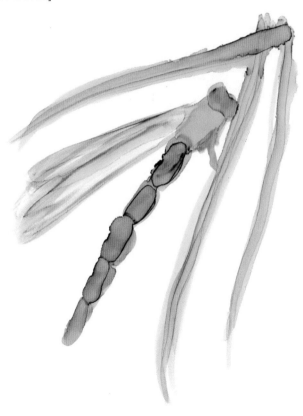

Who is allowed
To address
This thing that
Was created by us all
That affects us all

The answer is
Every one of us
In all our imperfections
Everyone

Surrendering over conquering
Cooperating over competing
Listening over leading

[Feminine Rising]

We worry about the economy
As if the economy is the water
That we drink to survive
As if it is the soil
Where we grow our food

Let us remember
That the economy is just an idea
And we can change ideas
If we want to

I made a list
Of the ways I try to
Be green
Be good

And I thought
That is not enough
Or maybe
I am not enough

[You Are Enough]

Let us not declare
A war on climate change
Annihilating greenhouse gases
And destroying polluters

Let us declare
A peaceful shift to better
A rising of nature lovers
An awakening of guardians
Because war is war

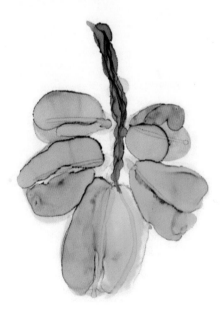

Step one
Fall in love with her
Step two
Treat her like you love her

[Two Step Solution]

I don't pretend to know
All the ways that
We can heal

Harness the energy
You use to complain
To help you transform

[Energy Conversion]

If we make this about sacrifice
If we make this about blame
If we make this about fear
If we make this about hate
Then we will lose

If we make this about together
If we make this about fun
If we make this about love
Then we will win

Taking care of
Someone you love versus
Taking care of
Someone you fear

[Act from Love]

Some pinecones
Need the fire
To spread the seed

It is so dark
We're going to have to
Feel our way
Out of this one

[Thinking is Overrated]

It is not science
That will save us

You don't need
To believe in magic
Only in healing

[Heal]

III

TRANSCENDENCE

Follow the children
They know the way
To tomorrow

She's loving
She's complex
She's ferocious and
She's absolutely stunning

[Gaia]

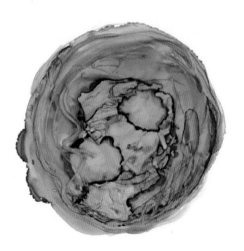

Call me crazy but I think
The solution lies somewhere
Within our favorite places
Those secret lakes or hills or streams

Where we stare at the rocks
And the trees and sky
And we know
Nothing we build
Could ever compare

Who doesn't
Love trees

[Trees Please]

Wild one
You were never meant
To live in a box
To dine on flesh and bones

Wild one
You were meant to be free
And eat fruit as you
Danced through your jungle home

Wild one
We gave you these plants
To eat and to heal and to enjoy
To hold the sun inside of you

Wild one
You have forgotten yourself
Find your plants and your peace
And remember

Our love for each other
Our love for ourselves
Our love for the planet

[Foundations]

Believe that
We can shrink our footprint
And expand our joy

You belong
You are powerful
You are uniquely beautiful

Be still sometimes
Be crazy sometimes
Be soft sometimes

Things take time
Things cycle and change
There is no such thing as the end

[Lessons from Nature]

It's so quiet
Here in the future

Every sunrise reminds us
To lighten up
For if the earth laughs in flowers
She must smile in sunshine

[Smile]

At some point I realized
I'm only ever as safe
As the goodwill of strangers together
I can only live in a world
As clean as we decide together

I give my heart to you
Because
The only way we can rise
Is if we rise together

She loves us
She loves us not
She loves us
She loves us not
She loves us

[She Loves Us]

In stillness
We can find solutions

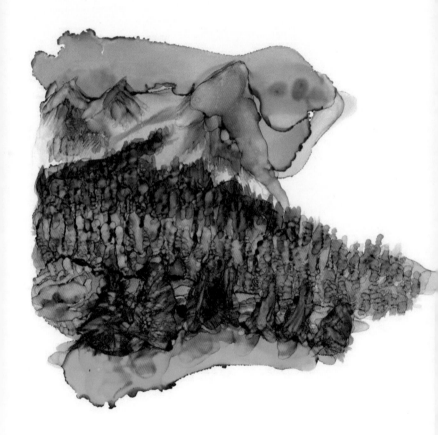

Be okay if it ends
Then it will all be okay
In the end

[In the End]

There is urgency and
There is time to
Breathe

Even after
All we will go through
I will still choose here

[Home]

Here we are again
Us humbled humans
Weird getting weirder
Little getting larger
Love getting louder

We are all waiting
To start doing this
And keep doing this
Together

Time to
Wake up our hearts
Tell a new story

Follow our joy and
Discover this
Beautiful new world

[Welcome]

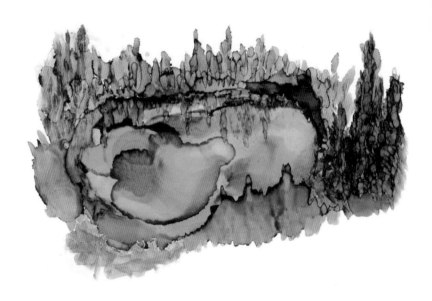

Note to the Reader

Dearest Reader,

Here we are together, in the midst of it all. This crucial, confusing, loud, and scary time. Or this beautiful, transformational, hopeful, and beloved time, depending on who you ask. I have been contemplating climate change for many years, and have had the opportunity to learn from many different teachers. Whenever I read laundry lists of how to reduce your carbon footprint, I always feel like something is missing. Something important.

I also often wonder, who gets to tell this story? This story of being on the brink: of a self-imposed doom called climate change. The scientists and the politicians can tell part of the story. The media and the activists can tell part of the story. And the writers, artists, and philosophers must tell part of the story as well.

Can we make it? Only time will tell. I am rooting for us.

Sending my love,
Nikki

About the Author

Nikki
She is a mother,
A poet,
An artist.
She is a homebody,
A book lover,
Plant eater.
When she laughs it echoes down every hallway,
She was raised near mountains and carries them in her
heart.

Printed in Great Britain
by Amazon